Healed from Idols

A
SCRIPTURE-BACKED
GUIDE ON HOW TO
READ THE BIBLE FOR
SPIRITUAL GROWTH

Chatassia Nu Grigsby

Followers of the Way

Copyright © 2021 by Chatassia Nu Grigsby

Scripture quotations are taken from the Holy Bible, New King James Version®. Copyright © 1982 by Thomas Nelson. Used by permission. All rights reserved.

All rights reserved. This book contains material protected under International and Federal Copyright Laws and Treaties. Any unauthorized reprint or use of this material is prohibited. No part of this book may be reproduced or transmitted in any form or by any means, electronic or mechanical, including photocopying, recording, or by any information storage and retrieval system without express written permission of the publisher, except in the case of brief quotations embodied in critical reviews and certain noncommercial uses permitted by copyright law.

Acknowledgments

I wish to acknowledge my Heavenly Father, King, and Elohim. I am truly astonished by your sovereignty and the love you have for me. I appreciate the gifts and assignments you have given me. I pray you continue to teach my hands and spirit to war because from the days of John the Baptist until now, the kingdom of heaven suffers violence, and the violent take it by force. I love you, and I pray I continue to make you proud.

* * *

I also wish to acknowledge and thank my loving husband and king, Quintarius, for being a spirit-led spouse, leader, and friend, whom God has anointed as an apostle and prophet. To witness your uncompromising faith and stance in the truth of God's Word is truly an inspiration. Your wisdom and integrity motivate me to continue to go beyond the basic principles of the knowledge of God.

It is truly an honor and privilege to be your wife and partner in advancing God's kingdom. I love you, and I pray I continue to make you proud.

As your saying goes in reference to your commitment to God's truth...

> *"You may buy me food.*
> *You may give me gifts.*
> *But you will not change my mind."*

Contents

1	Introduction	1
2	Why Should I Read the Bible?	4
3	Why Is the Bible Dreadful to Read for Many?	9
4	Justification and Sanctification Is Essential For Salvation	11
5	What About Being Justified by Faith in Jesus Alone?	15
6	What Happens When I Rely on Faith in Jesus Without Works?	18
7	Final Conditioning of Mind and Spirit Prior to Reading	21
8	Which Bible Translation Should I Read?	25
9	Where to Begin Reading?	29
10	Spiritual Maturity and Stagnation's Effects	33
11	What Hinders Me from Growing In God's Word?	36

12 Conclusion of the Matter 40

Epilogue 43
Suggested Resources 45

1

Introduction

The God of Israel or YHWH[1] (Jesus' or Yahshua's[2] Father) has always commanded His people not to partake in idolatry and only worship Him. Idols are not only the worship of a person, image, or object as if it is God; idols are anyone or anything that takes the place of God in one's life. It is an idol, whether it is excessive admiration for a pastor, a wooden object that one worships, false conceptions of God, or excessive time spent on social media that results in a lack of devout fellowship with Him. God forbids idolatry because it strikes the heart of the relationship between Him and His people.

John 4:24 states, "God *is* Spirit, and those who worship Him must worship in spirit and truth."[3] Those who have received Jesus as Lord and Savior, He has blessed with the gift of the Holy Spirit, which is the instrument that allows humanity access to God for worship and fellowship; the Spirit also assists with the spiritual maturation process. In addition to worshipping God in spirit, God must also be worshipped in the sincerity of His truth. Jesus states that God's Word is truth (John 17:17). His people's thoughts and behaviors must align with His Word or truth.

God's Word is also His commandments or instructions for living. It is through obeying His instructions is how God's people show that they worship and love Him. Observe Jesus' words:

> *If you love Me, keep My commandments.*
> *-John 14:15*
> *As the Father loved Me, I also have loved you; abide in My love. If you keep My commandments, you will abide in My love, just as I have kept My Father's commandments and abide in His love.*
> *-John 15:9-10*

These scriptures may seem foreign or terrifying, but contrary to popular teachings, this has always been God's standard and love language: keeping His commandments. Many people refrain from teaching or speaking about this truth because they believe it will take away from the significance of Jesus' atoning sacrifice; however, it serves as a disadvantage to those who desire to have a legitimate relationship with God and obtain salvation since willful sin and disobedience separate them from Him.

This short book uses scriptural evidence to debunk idolatrous misconceptions about God, Jesus, and salvation that hinder one from reading and maturing in God's Word. It also provides guidance on how to approach the Bible mentally and where to begin reading it. Whether newly converted in Christ or seasoned in Christ, this book serves as a Scripture-backed guide to reading the Bible for spiritual maturity and life-long study unto salvation.

Before diving into where to begin reading the Bible, it is essential that we condition the mind to approach the Bible appropriately for spiritual growth. Because of this, I encourage you to read this book completely and in sequential order.

---

[1]YHWH is God's name in Hebrew. It is typically written out as Yahuah (pronounced Yah-hoo-ah). It means the name of Elohim (God), which is the Almighty Creator of the heavens and the earth.

[2]Yahshua (pronounced Yah-shoo-ah) is Jesus Christ's original name in Hebrew.

[3]Scripture quotations are taken from the New King James Version (NKJV).

2

Why Should I Read the Bible?

God's Word serves as life's essential guide to fulfilling His purpose for creating the heavens, earth, and humanity: to establish His kingdom on earth through the human race spreading its rule as His image-bearers as all creation praise and worship Him in spirit and truth. Because of this, humanity is purposed with significant responsibility in advancing God's kingdom.

Do you think it is rational to acquire a job and not receive instructions, training, or guidance on completing what is required from your employer? Neither do I!

Through His Word, God has given us instructions that equip us to complete the work we have been assigned to do. In Ephesians 2:10, Apostle Paul states, "For we are His workmanship, created in Christ Jesus for good works, which God prepared beforehand that we should walk in them."

The Bible should be read because the more informed one is about the significance of their work, the more equipped and willing they will be to complete their work.

Paul wrote that all Scripture was written for us to learn, have hope, be rebuked, corrected, and instructed in righteousness to be equipped for every good work:

> *For whatever things were written before were written for our learning, that we through the patience and comfort of the Scriptures might have hope.*
> ***-Romans 15:4***
>
> *All Scripture is given by inspiration of God, and is profitable for doctrine, for reproof, for correction, for instruction in righteousness, that the man of God may be complete, thoroughly equipped for every good work.*
> ***-2 Timothy 3:16-17***

When one obtains a job, it is befitting to be compensated for completing their job functions; likewise, it is also befitting to be terminated for not completing their job functions. Well, God has a compensation plan for humanity, whether one works for Him or not.

His compensation plan details that there are blessings for obedience and curses for disobedience. This detailed plan was first introduced in the book of Leviticus. It can be found in Leviticus 26 and Deuteronomy 28. This compensation plan was initially administered to the Hebrews as a guide for holy living after God had delivered them from the bondage of slavery in

Egypt. Although the plan was addressed to an original Hebrew audience, it is still helpful to humanity today because it helps distinguish right from wrong and holy from unholy.

Additionally, the guide highlights God's utter love for obedience and utter hate for disobedience—which is still His sentiment today. Romans 6:23 states, "For the wages of sin *is* death, but the gift of God *is* eternal life in Christ Jesus our Lord." If one completes their job functions in Jesus Christ, they will be compensated with eternal life; however, if they defy their job functions by continuously sinning outside of Christ, they will be compensated with eternal death.

The Bible should be read because it is humanity's employment handbook, which is a detailed overview of the policy specific to the kingdom of God; it includes procedures, guidelines, benefits, and consequences for living in accordance with the job functions. Reading the Bible is essential for being equipped to fulfill one's job obligations.

Most importantly, biblical text highlights humanity's need for Christ, the Savior, and it provides guidance on remaining in Him and receiving the compensation of eternal life instead of eternal death. Jesus states that unless one abides in Him, they can not do anything, making it impossible to complete their job functions. Therefore, reading the Bible is not an option.

> *Abide in Me, and I in you. As the branch cannot bear fruit of itself, unless it abides in the vine, neither can you, unless you abide in Me. "I am the vine, you are the branches. He who abides in Me, and I in him, bears much fruit; for without Me you can do nothing. If*

anyone does not abide in Me, he is cast out as a branch and is withered; and they gather them and throw them into the fire, and they are burned.
-John 15:4-6

There is therefore now no condemnation to those who are in Christ Jesus, who do not walk according to the flesh, but according to the Spirit.
-Romans 8:1

BUT WHAT ABOUT MY INDIVIDUALITY?

It is a common belief that God desires to strip people of their identities completely. This belief is true in the sense that He desires to uproot sinful roots that give birth to false identities and other falsehoods; however, it is far from the truth when it comes to an individual's nature and personality. I do not imply that a poor attitude and wicked behavior are permissible because He will cultivate a person as they are sanctified and developed through His Word. I am saying that God will work through an individual's nature and personality, despite their imperfections, in a way that will glorify Him.

In fact, Bible scholars use the term "organic inspiration" to denote the Holy Spirit used the personalities, experiences, outlooks, and intentions of biblical authors as He supervised and directed their writings. Therefore, the Holy Spirit can supervise and direct you as a vessel of honor as well, but you must yield your life to God's Word.

Jesus says if we try to save our life, we will lose it, but if we lose it for Him, we will find it. I wholeheartedly attest to this truth:

> *For whoever desires to save his life will lose it, but whoever loses his life for My sake will find it.*
> ***-Matthew 16:25***
> *He who finds his life will lose it, and he who loses his life for My sake will find it.*
> ***-Matthew 10:39***

3

Why Is the Bible Dreadful to Read for Many?

I am certain that for many people, the Bible is one of the most dreaded books to read for various reasons. One of the main reasons is that the Bible is perceived as the supreme and divine book of rules that tells humanity everything they should not do and what they should do. Because of this, it highlights the sin in their lives and reveals how wretched and fallible humanity is in the flesh. This realization often overwhelm people in such a way that they feel that their history with sin and need for spiritual cleansing is so profound that it is difficult to see themselves in a renewed state. In light of biblical standards, they often become discouraged by the transformative work that needs to be done within them to see themselves as one that biblical text describes as righteous rather than wicked. This perception causes many to become defeated and alienated from God in their minds and hearts, so they give up on reading the Bible entirely.

For the sake of time, whether the reason for not reading biblical text is due to one's lack of discipline, comprehensive confidence, unruly lifestyle, doubts, or any other factor, reading the Bible is not optional. More specifically, it is not optional for those who can comprehensively read and hope to obtain final salvation by faith in being justified through Jesus Christ's atoning sacrifice.

If one desires fellowship with God now and after death, they must understand the only way this is possible: "Jesus said to him, "I am the way, the truth, and the life. No one comes to the Father except through Me" (John 14:6). One can only be reconciled to the Father, both now and unto the culmination of Christ, is through Jesus Christ.

Through Christ's atoning sacrifice, those who receive Him as their Lord and Savior, by faith, will be justified before a Holy God. However, they must undergo the process of sanctification unto final salvation.

4

Justification and Sanctification Is Essential For Salvation

Throughout this book, I will be reiterating "salvation in its entirety" to emphasize that salvation is a process. To verify it is a process, Jesus states that salvation is to those who endure until the end: "But he who endures to the end shall be saved" (Matthew 24:13).

Justification is the legal declaration that acquits a sinner from the guilt of their sin; it credits them with the righteousness of Christ. In justification, God declares people as righteous and just due to Jesus' atoning work; a new legal status is constituted to them.

The doctrine of justification is a concept that has been incorrectly taught and misunderstood for centuries. I am convinced that because of this, innumerable people are at risk of not obtaining salvation in its entirety. The improper teaching and understanding have led many to believe that if they believe or have faith alone in Jesus as Lord and Savior (in the absence of sanctification), they will be justified before a Holy God and obtain salvation in its entirety.

Once one has received God's Word or Jesus and becomes regenerated from a state of spiritual death to spiritual life, by the working of the Holy Spirit, justification, sanctification, and salvation are initially imputed to them. However, in response to being regenerated, one must be converted by yielding themself to the Holy Spirit and allowing their thoughts and behaviors to align with the essence of God's Word that they received when they were initially regenerated. The convert's thoughts and actions must validate their new life and belief (sanctification).

Sanctification is a work of God by the Holy Spirit in those who have been regenerated and converted that continually works within one to make them holy or sanctify them. However, human effort is required. The "let go and let God" mentality that implies there is an inactive role in being sanctified is unbiblical.

Sanctification should never be confused with justification; however, they will never function properly without the other. God commands His people to be holy because He is holy:

> *For I am the Lord who brings you up out of the land of Egypt, to be your God. You shall therefore be holy, for I am holy.*
> **-Leviticus 11:45**

> *But as He who called you is holy, you also be holy in all your conduct, because it is written, "Be holy, for I am holy.*
> *-1 Peter 1:15-16*

When we think of salvation, it is vital to understand that it is a *process* to the gates of heaven for complete reign and unity with the Most High God. This process requires progressive workings of the Holy Spirit along with human effort.

Salvation includes aspects of being called, regenerated, converted, justified, adopted, sanctified, perseverance in the faith, and final glorification. Contrary to the popular "Once saved, always saved" teaching, salvation is a process; it is a state of "accomplished" and "to be accomplished or "now" and "not yet".

Paul encouraged the converted, faithful Philippians to work out their salvation:

> *Therefore, my beloved, as you have always obeyed, not as in my presence only, but now much more in my absence, work out your salvation with fear and trembling; for it is God who works in you both to will and to do for His good pleasure.*
> *-Philippians 2:12-13*

The process of salvation, including a justified status, requires maintenance; this maintenance or upkeep is obtained through being sanctified through God's Word by the Holy Spirit and human effort.

Paul affirms this conditional justification, sanctification, and salvation:

> *And you, who once were alienated and enemies in your mind by wicked works, yet now He has reconciled in the body of His flesh through death, to present you holy, and blameless, and above reproach in His sight—* ***if indeed you continue in the faith, grounded and steadfast, and are not moved away from the hope of the gospel*** *which you heard, which was preached to every creature under heaven, of which I, Paul, became a minister.*
> **-Colossians 1:21-23**

5

What About Being Justified by Faith in Jesus Alone?

While believing or having faith in Jesus to be justified for salvation is irrefutably true, the quality of the faith or belief by way of sanctification will determine if one will be justified before a Holy God and obtain salvation in its entirety. In the Bible, there are passages where Paul mentions being justified and saved through faith in Jesus alone, and there is a passage where James, Jesus' brother, teaches that faith without works is dead. These two notions may seem contradictory to one another; however, they are not. They must be viewed as statements regarding pre-conversion and post-conversion. For example, to be regenerated from a state of spiritual death to spiritual life, one must have faith in Jesus alone to be saved (pre-conversion).

Once one has been regenerated, to continue being justified and obtain salvation in its entirety, they must have faith and works (post-conversion); their works (thoughts and behaviors) must validate their faith, which develops sanctification.

Let us go further. Paul states in Galatians 2:16, "Knowing that a man is not justified by the works of the law but by faith in Jesus Christ, even we have believed in Christ Jesus, that we might be justified by faith in Christ and not by the works of the law; for by the works of the law no flesh shall be justified." Paul's audience was Judaizers who were teaching Gentile believers that their obedience to the Jewish laws were the grounds for justification. His statement has been tragically misconstrued for generations and used as a tool to deceive people into believing that belief or faith alone (absence of works or sanctification) will justify and reconcile them to God unto final salvation. Paul meant that works are not the grounds for justification because Jesus is the only ground. In fact, according to Isaiah 64:6, man's righteousness is filthy rags to God. Jesus is the only point of access to God.

Fortunately, James provides clarity on what the substance of saving faith is. The second chapter of James dismantled the "If you believe or have faith in Jesus alone (without good works or sanctification), you will be saved." notion. He states, "You believe that there is one God. You do well. Even the demons believe—and tremble" (James 2:19). I am sure Satan and his demons believe in all aspects of the Bible in a sense; however, they still will not be justified or saved.

What makes them different from those who are on track to obtaining final salvation? It is their wicked and disobedient works, thoughts, and behaviors that set them apart. This fact tells us that it takes more than mere knowledge or belief in Jesus to be justified and saved.

In James 2:26, he states, "For as the body without the spirit is dead, so faith without works is dead also." Works are the quality of faith. It is through works that one's faith is justified: "But someone will say, 'You have faith, and I have works.' Show me your faith without your works, and I will show you my faith by my works" (James 2:18). A faith that saves must work; the work is evidence of what one believes, and it produces sanctification: good thoughts and behaviors that align with God's Word.

Without faith in Jesus to be saved, there is no justification since justification is by faith in Him alone. Without works, there is no faith because faith without works is dead. Therefore, without faith and works, there is no justification and sanctification, which are essential for salvation in its entirety. It is impossible for justification and sanctification to function properly without the other.

Jesus' atoning work does not supersede human responsibility to obey God's Word unto final salvation; there is no way around it.

6

What Happens When I Rely on Faith in Jesus Without Works?

Jesus affirms that many who think they will enter the kingdom of heaven because of Him will not achieve that:

> *Not everyone who says to Me, 'Lord, Lord,' shall enter the kingdom of heaven, but he who does the will of My Father in heaven. Many will say to Me in that day, 'Lord, Lord, have we not prophesied in Your name, cast out demons in Your name, and done many wonders in Your name?' And then I will declare to them, 'I never knew you; depart from Me, you who practice lawlessness.*

-Matthew 7:21-23

The fact that people will not obtain salvation in its entirety despite doing wonders in His name begs acknowledgment of why salvation will not be granted.

Jesus states that those who do the will of His Father will enter the kingdom of heaven. In other words, those who perform their job functions according to God's Word will enter the kingdom of heaven. The criteria for obtaining salvation in its entirety requires more than sole belief in His name; it requires belief in the fullness of His name, which motivates one's thoughts, actions, and behaviors to do the will of His Father in Heaven. A live faith that works is the way of salvation.

It must be seared in mind that Jesus says, "Do not think that I came to destroy the Law or the Prophets. I did not come to destroy but to fulfill" (Matthew 5:17). Though many disregard the Old Testament and focus solely on the New Testament, Jesus' fulfillment of the Law and the Prophets was never meant to supersede humanity's responsibility to obey God and uphold His standards for living. Regardless of humanity's incapability to be perfectly obedient to God, obedience to God's instructions for living has always been and will always be His will and standard.

After all, that is why Jesus was the perfect sacrifice; He was obedient unto death. He performed His duty, and humanity must perform theirs. Jesus states, "Strive to enter through the narrow gate, for many, I say to you, will seek to enter and will not be able" (Luke 13:24). Jesus is saying just ***try and make great efforts*** to enter through the narrow gate. Sadly, many will not enter through the narrow gate because of their lack of consistently trying to be obedient to God's instructions.

I encourage you to shift to or maintain a proper perspective regarding reading and applying God's Word. Instead of regarding it as an entity that limits your life by telling you what you should not do, regard God's Word as life's essential guidebook that sanctifies you unto salvation in its entirety. After all, we cannot live any better than we know how to live.

Jesus prayed to God for His disciples: "Sanctify them by Your truth. Your word is truth" (John 17:17). God's truth must sanctify you to produce good works that validate your faith in Jesus.

7

Final Conditioning of Mind and Spirit Prior to Reading

Now that you understand that reading the Bible and having sanctified works is not an option if you desire to obtain salvation in its entirety, let us discuss the final way you must approach the Bible. It is vital that you refrain from choosing which mandates you want to subscribe to over others. You must not choose to accept and apply what is convenient for you and sin. If you find it challenging to receive His Word at times, ask Him to help you accept and apply it because the times and our desires may change, but His Word and standard of obedience endures forever.

You must understand and accept that the Word of God is going to convict you. It may even hurt your feelings at times. Therefore, you must keep this in mind:

> *For the word of God is living and powerful, and sharper than any two-edged sword, piercing even to the division of soul and spirit, and of joints and marrow, and is a discerner of the thoughts and intents of the heart.*
> **-Hebrews 4:12**

God's Word cuts and destroys, but it also heals and rebuilds. Do not give up on the process; persevere.

REPENTANCE

Before reading biblical text, I encourage you to examine yourself. You are about to read Holy Scriptures, and you need the Holy Spirit to teach you. If there are any surface sins you have committed, begin repenting of those sins first. Then search within yourself for other deep and hidden sins to repent of. Practice repentance daily so that it becomes a lifestyle. For the sake of clarity, repentance is not solely saying, "Lord, please forgive me for my sins." without a renewed commitment to renounce the sins. Repentance is a change of mind that requires turning away from the sin committed with a renewed commitment that produces actions or evidence of the repented sin.

Here are scriptures that you can use as a prayer to petition God for a clean heart and an unwavering spirit that searches your soul for the sake of purification and sanctification:

Create in me a clean heart, O God, And renew a steadfast spirit within me.
-Psalm 51:10
Search me, O God, and know my heart; Try me, and know my anxieties; And see if there is any wicked way in me, And lead me in the way everlasting.
-Psalm 139:23-24

Repentance yields deliverance from sin and strongholds that will make you unfruitful and devour you if left unaddressed.

PRAY FOR WISDOM

The Holy Spirit is a helper and teacher (John 14:26), so you do not have to rely on your sole interpretation of biblical text. Pray that God gives you the spirit of wisdom and revelation of the knowledge of Him and the eyes of your understanding be enlightened (Ephesians 1:17-18). You may use this as a quicker prayer: "Father, please give me wisdom, knowledge, and understanding of your holy Word, and teach me how to apply it. In Yahshua's (Jesus') name. Amen."

Here is a passage, written by Paul, that relates to praying for spiritual wisdom:

> *Therefore I also, after I heard of your faith in the Lord Jesus and your love for all the saints, do not cease to give thanks for you, making mention of you in my prayers: that the God of our Lord Jesus Christ, the Father of glory, may give to you the spirit of wisdom and revelation in the knowledge of Him, the eyes of your understanding being enlightened; that you may know what is the hope of His calling, what are the riches of the glory of His inheritance in the saints, and what is the exceeding greatness of His power toward us who believe, according to the working of His mighty power which He worked in Christ when He raised Him from the dead and seated Him at His right hand in the heavenly places, far above all principality and power and might and dominion, and every name that is named, not only in this age but also in that which is to come. And He put all things under His feet, and gave Him to be head over all things to the church, which is His body, the fullness of Him who fills all in all.*
> *-Ephesians 1:15-21*

8

Which Bible Translation Should I Read?

The Old Testament is originally known as the Tanakh; it was written in Hebrew (some Aramaic), and the New Testament was written in Greek. They both comprise what we now call the Bible. To read and understand the words within the original manuscripts, one must know how to read Hebrew, Aramaic, and Greek. However, for those who do not, they must settle for translated versions of the original manuscripts.

I recommend that you select a Bible translation that you can easily read and understand. Since there are many Bible translations, I will provide you with the three *types* of translations: Formal Equivalent (Literal or Word-for-Word), Dynamic

Equivalent (Thought-for-Thought), and Free Translation (Paraphrased).

A Formal equivalent or word-for-word translation's goal is to remain as close as possible to words and phrases used in the original manuscripts. Where possible, this translation attempts to find single English words to reflect each Hebrew, Aramaic, or Greek word used in the original manuscripts. It seeks to preserve the original word order as possible, even if its style is awkward. These translations are often more challenging to read or understand.

Here are some translations:

- NASB — New American Standard Bible
- KJV — King James Version
- NKJV — New King James Version
- AMP — Amplified Bible
- ESV — English Standard Version

A Dynamic Equivalent or thought-for-thought translation aims to accommodate the modern reader's language, making it more natural and less awkward. It seeks to find precise equivalents for the original manuscripts' words, expressions, and grammatical constructions that produce the closest equivalent in both meaning and style. It attempts to keep historical and factual matters intact. However, seeking to accommodate the modern reader increases the historical distance some, allowing more opportunities for translators' opinions to come forth.

Here are some translations:

- NIV — New International Version
- CSB — Christian Standard Bible
- NAB — New American Bible
- NLT — New Living Translation
- CEV — Contemporary English Version

A Functional Equivalent or Paraphrase translation's goal is to paraphrase the ideas in the original manuscripts to be easily read in modern language. This translation should be used to grasp a story or passage's flow further; it should not be relied on to accurately determine the meaning of any text.

Here are some translations:

- MSG — The Message
- CEV — Contemporary English Version
- LB — The Living Bible

When I first began journeying with the Lord, I used the New International Version (NIV), a Dynamic Equivalent or thought-for-thought translation. I did not know the types of Bible translations; I just knew I could not read my grandmother's preferred translation, King James Version (KJV). I found the NIV to be more approachable. The NIV significantly helped me as I grew in the faith during the first years. I still find myself quoting some of my favorite scriptures in the NIV.

However, as I grew in God's Word, I transitioned to the KJV. I currently use the KJV and NKJV (New King James Version). These two translations have helped me become a more keen Bible scholar. The NIV, KJV, and NKJV have significantly impacted my spiritual development. I am sharing this to encourage you to choose a translation that works best for you.

If you do not see the translation you use listed, search to discover the translation type to serve you better. I also recommend that you compare versions of Scripture to determine distinctions as you study biblical text.

Remember:

> *All Scripture is given by inspiration of God, and is profitable for doctrine, for reproof, for correction, for instruction in righteousness, that the man of God may be complete, thoroughly equipped for every good work.*
> **-2 Timothy 3:16-17**

9

Where to Begin Reading?

You must keep in mind that although the Bible was written for us today, it still has an original audience and context. The author, original audience, and context of that time must be considered when reading the Bible. Knowing this will help you interpret Scripture more accurately and enhance your understanding. Even if you have to do a quick Google search to discover this information, it is worth it. Some Study Bibles have this information including the purpose of the author's book before the beginning of each chapter. I have included the Study Bible I use in the Suggested Resources section of this book.

Ultimately, I recommend that you read the Bible as the Spirit leads you and based on what you and your spirit needs such as wisdom, strength, encouragement, peace, hope, patience, etc.; however, for the sake of a starting point, I suggest you begin reading in the New Testament, which opens with the four Gospels (Good News): Matthew, Mark, Luke, and John. However, I encourage you to read John first because, in addition to providing an eyewitness account of the life of Jesus, he also provides theological content on faith in Jesus for salvation.

Each author of the four gospels presents the same narrative of the coming of God's kingdom, so do not be surprised when you encounter statements stated in a previous chapter. However, they used their unique personalities, perspectives, and concerns to write their narratives. Each gospel describes the same Jesus, speaks about Him in different ways, and highlights different aspects of His ministry.

As you venture forward reading the Bible, I recommend you be intentional about completing each book you begin reading. If you can, try to complete each chapter or book in one sitting, but if it is not possible, strive to complete the remaining chapters when you are next available. Remember: it is also important to be led by the Spirit to read what you and your spirit need, so do not feel pressured to always complete entire books.

Nevertheless, I will give you a reason why you should be intentional about reading entire books. Let us put in mind Apostle Paul; he wrote various epistles (letters) addressed to churches in the New Testament. In each epistle, Paul wrote to address specific issues that arose in the churches. I want you to imagine that you have received an email or letter from someone you highly respect. It could be a loved one, mentor, manager, colleague, etc., that you desire to be perceived in a positive light because you have great respect for them as a leader. Once you begin reading the message, you notice they are not saying favorable words about you, so you stop reading the message. However, if you had continued reading, you would have read positive and encouraging remarks about doing well. Likewise, if you read only the middle or end of the message, you would miss out on information that would correct and teach you. As a result, you would miss out on growth and development opportunities. You needed to read the entire message to understand and receive its full essence.

I have given this illustration to show that you must read Paul's epistles in their entirety to get accurate knowledge and understanding of his complete message to his audience. This concept further applies to how you must be intentional about completing books of the Bible to strive to get the most accurate interpretation and understanding of the Bible's messaging.

OLD TESTAMENT

There is a notion held by many people who believe there is no reason for reading the Old Testament because we now have the New Testament. This idea is far from the truth; I will even say it is idolatrous and blasphemous. To start, we must acknowledge that the Old Testament, or Tanakh, was Jesus' and the early church's only "Bible". That is why you will notice authors often quoting from the Old Testament or Tanakh with the introduction, "For it is written". Jesus even affirmed the Old

Testament by saying, "Do not think that I came to destroy the Law or the Prophets. I did not come to destroy but to fulfill. For assuredly, I say to you, till heaven and earth pass away, one jot or one tittle will by no means pass from the law till all is fulfilled" (Matthew 5:17-18). The Old Testament points to Christ and contains prophecies that have not been fulfilled yet. Neglecting the Old Testament is dangerous because it considerably influences our understanding of teachings in both the Old and New Testaments.

Although there have been some historical and cultural developments, we must also acknowledge that this current world we live in is the same as those of the Old Testament lived in. Similarly, we are the same kind of people: sinful, persecuted, and bound to God by covenant. We also experience the judgments of blessings and curses by the same unchanging God as them. He's a covenant-keeping God, so relationships with Him are based on covenant. Fortunately for us, we have access to their history to learn from them. Paul states, "Now all these things happened to them as examples, and they were written for our admonition, upon whom the ends of the ages have come" (1 Corinthians 10:11). As the adage goes, "You do not have to touch fire to know you will get burned." We can learn from the characters of the Old Testament's mistakes and also receive encouragement from their stories of faith, obedience, and perseverance.

The Old Testament helps us to better understand the big picture: God's work in history to establish His kingdom on earth through the human race spreading its rule as His image-bearers as all creation praise and worship Him in spirit and truth.

10

Spiritual Maturity and Stagnation's Effects

Apostle Paul encourages spiritual maturity: going beyond the basic principles and teachings about Christ and God's Word (Hebrews 5:12-14). He parallels people who are stagnant in basic teachings with a baby who still consumes milk. Paul states that although they should be teachers by now, they still need someone to reteach them the basic principles. Moreover, he states that the solid food of God's Word is for the full aged because they have put it to exercise and can discern good from evil. Since spiritually mature people put God's Word to practice, they can be vessels of honor who can teach others the basics of God's Word.

For though by this time you ought to be teachers,
you need someone to teach you again the first principles

> *of the oracles of God; and you have come to need milk and not solid food. For everyone who partakes only of milk is unskilled in the word of righteousness, for he is a babe. But solid food belongs to those who are of full age, that is, those who by reason of use have their senses exercised to discern both good and evil.*
> **-Hebrews 5:12-14**

Paul also warns of the perils of not progressing to mature in God's Word (Hebrews 6:1-8). One only has a chance to do better if they know better, so they will not do better if they do not strive to know better. Additionally, he warns against apostasy, a refusal to continue to follow and obey God and His Word:

> *Therefore, leaving the discussion of the elementary principles of Christ, let us go on to perfection, not laying again the foundation of repentance from dead works and of faith toward God, of the doctrine of baptisms, of laying on of hands, of resurrection of the dead, and of eternal judgment. And this we will do if God permits. For it is impossible for those who were once enlightened, and have tasted the heavenly gift, and have become partakers of the Holy Spirit, and have tasted the good word of God and the powers of the age to come, if they fall away, to renew them again to repentance, since they crucify again for themselves the Son of God, and put Him to an open shame. For the*

> *earth which drinks in the rain that often comes upon it, and bears herbs useful for those by whom it is cultivated, receives blessing from God; but if it bears thorns and briers, it is rejected and near to being cursed, whose end is to be burned.*
> *-Hebrews 6:1-8*

Contrary to today's culture that approves and glorify Godless living because "Jesus has paid it all, and all will be forgiven.", Paul says Jesus is no longer a sacrifice for those who willfully sin despite coming into the truth of God's Word:

> *For if we sin wilfully after that we have received the knowledge of the truth, there remaineth no more sacrifice for sins, But a certain fearful looking for of judgment and fiery indignation, which shall devour the adversaries.*
> *-Hebrews 10:26-27*

The freedom we have in Christ is to be free from the bondage of sin and granted eternal life; this freedom is not to fulfill our fleshly desires, which yield eternal death. There is no profit in gaining the whole world but losing our souls (Mark 8:36).

11

What Hinders Me from Growing In God's Word?

The Word of God teaches us to be doers of the Word and not hearers only. It is not sufficient to hear and read the Word without application. James states that a person who does not apply the Word that has been implanted is like one who looks at themselves in the mirror and immediately forgets what they look like:

> *But be doers of the word, and not hearers only, deceiving yourselves. For if anyone is a hearer of the word and not a doer, he is like a man observing his natural face in a mirror; for he observes himself, goes*

> *away, and immediately forgets what kind of man he was. But he who looks into the perfect law of liberty and continues in it, and is not a forgetful hearer but a doer of the work, this one will be blessed in what he does.*
> **-James 1:22-25**

In contrast, he states that those who are hearers and doers of God's instruction will be blessed in what they do. There are always rewards on the other side of obedience, whether tangible or intangible. We must continue in God's Word consistently.

God's Word consistently tells us not to love this world and the things within it. It commands us not to conform to its patterns but instead be transformed by our minds being renewed so that we can prove God's good, acceptable, and perfect will (Romans 12:2).

John affirms this notion with this warning:

> *Do not love the world or the things in the world. If anyone loves the world, the love of the Father is not in him. For all that is in the world—the lust of the flesh, the lust of the eyes, and the pride of life—is not of the Father but is of the world. And the world is passing away, and the lust of it; but he who does the will of God abides forever.*
> **-1 John 2:15-17**

Loving this world by sharing the same thoughts, cares, and behaviors as it hinders one from growing in the Word and being fruitful: "Now he who received seed among the thorns is he who hears the word, and the cares of this world and the deceitfulness of riches choke the word, and he becomes unfruitful" (Matthew 13:22).

To grow in God's Word and be fruitful, one must be a consistent hearer, reader, and doer of it. Peter tells what must be added to not be barren or unfruitful in growing in the knowledge of the Lord:

> *But also for this very reason, giving all diligence, add to your faith virtue, to virtue knowledge, to knowledge self-control, to self-control perseverance, to perseverance godliness, to godliness brotherly kindness, and to brotherly kindness love. For if these things are yours and abound, you will be neither barren nor unfruitful in the knowledge of our Lord Jesus Christ. For he who lacks these things is shortsighted, even to blindness, and has forgotten that he was cleansed from his old sins.*
> **-Peter 2:5-9**

There must be progressive sanctification taking place for you to mature in God's Word. Therefore, partaking in sinful and wicked behavior is sure to hinder progression. There are no shortcuts to growing in God's Word apart from submission and obedience to it.

PRAY AND READ EVERY DAY

I will admit that there may be times when you absolutely do not feel like praying or reading. When this happens, I encourage you to pray that God ignites your zeal for praying and reading His Word while removing anything hindering you from doing so.

I find this method effective when this happens to me: the book of Proverbs, wisdom literature, has 31 chapters. There are usually 30-31 days each month, so whatever day it is, I read the chapter for that day. For example, if the day is January 15th, I will read Proverbs 15. After all, Proverbs 4:7 states, "Wisdom is the principal thing; therefore get wisdom: and with all thy getting get understanding."

When you find it difficult to pray, consider fasting or talking to the Lord through journaling to Him. You must do whatever you have to do to keep the line of communication open.

12

Conclusion of the Matter

One of my greatest prayers is that you are healed from idolatrous and false concepts about God, Jesus, and salvation that hinder you from reading and maturing in God's Word. I pray you understand how significant your work in establishing God's kingdom on earth is and that the Bible is your guidebook to fulfilling your job functions. I pray you thoroughly understand that salvation is a process that requires your active participation, so reading and developing through and by God's Word is not an option. The only way to obtain salvation in its entirety is through faith in Jesus **and** being sanctified through God's Word until the end. I also pray you have greater confidence in approaching and reading the Bible.

This book serves as a condensed guide to assist with your *personal* journey of spiritual development through reading the

Bible and hopefully beyond it (such as other literature and books that have been excluded). I must note that additional literature must never deny the Father, Son, or Holy Spirit. There is always more to learn to enhance your understanding of the Bible, so please do not limit yourself!

As you venture forward developing in God's Word, you will fall short of His glory sometimes and experience difficult times. Romans 8:1 states, "There is therefore now no condemnation to those who are in Christ Jesus, who do not walk according to the flesh, but according to the Spirit." Although there are consequences for every positive and negative action, you will not be condemned to eternal death if you sin while consistently striving to walk according to the Spirit. However, be sure to repent with a renewed commitment that strives not to repeat the sin.

It is also important to note that as you venture forward developing in God's Word, you will notice more opposition and spiritual warfare because you will be awakened. Satan desires you to remain asleep and unaware. You will also be tried and tested by God to assess your faith and development for the sake of your continued growth and sanctification. Therefore, every obstacle will not be a "Get behind me, Satan." obstacle. Sometimes you will also experience God's judgment to rebuke, correct, and reconcile you back to Him. I encourage you to seek the Lord for wisdom during those times to learn and be equipped both in season and out of season to overcome tests and trials.

King Solomon is deemed the wisest and wealthiest man who ever lived. In his book, Ecclesiastes, he wrote to spare future generations the bitterness of learning how life outside of God is meaningless through their own life's experiences. He closed his final chapter with these words, and they will also serve as the final words of mine:

> *Let us hear the conclusion of the whole matter: Fear God and keep His commandments, For this is man's all. For God will bring every work into judgment, Including every secret thing, Whether good or evil.*
> **-*Ecclesiastes 12:13-14***

Epilogue

You have been commanded to love the Lord, your God with all your heart, soul, and mind. I pray you keep Jesus' love language stored within your heart. He states, "If you love me, keep my commandments" (John 14:15). I pray you love God by striving to keep His commandments while hating evil. I pray you do not use your liberty in Christ to sin willfully.

I pray you never compromise the truth for a lie and lovingly correct others when they believe and behave as though faith in Christ is passive instead of active. As we know, it is the works that validate the faith. I pray you continue in God's perfect law of liberty so that even those outside of the faith may take notice, see your good works, and glorify your Father in heaven.

Now, I leave you with the Great Commission that Jesus commissioned to His disciples, which also includes you:

> *Go therefore and make disciples of all the nations, baptizing them in the name of the Father and of the Son and of the Holy Spirit, teaching them to observe all things that I have commanded you; and lo, I am with you always, even to the end of the age. Amen.*

Matthew 28:19-20

Suggested Resources

The Holy Bible (your preferred translation)

The *Life Application Study Bible* by Tyndale House Publishers (your preferred translation)

If *Healed From Idols: A Scripture-Backed Guide on How* to Read the Bible for Spiritual Growth has proven to be valuable to you, please recommend it to others.

www.ingramcontent.com/pod-product-compliance
Lightning Source LLC
Chambersburg PA
CBHW032338300426
44109CB00041B/1279